# ABOUT SK
# MATH GRADE 7

MW00587996

## BY JERRY ATEN

The Skill Builders series features a variety of fun and challenging workbooks designed to provide students with extra practice on basic skills. Exercises are grade-appropriate and based on national standards to help ensure that students master the skills they need the most.

Skill Builders *Math Grade 7* provides students with focused practice to help reinforce and develop math skills. This book provides grade-level appropriate activities and clear instructions. The exercises cover a variety of math skills, including algebra, data analysis, geometry, and measurement. In addition, a diagnostic test helps identify areas where students need additional practice and instruction.

Skill Builders are available for a variety of subject areas and grade levels to help students master grade-level skills or prepare them for the grade ahead.

**Credits:**
Editor: Julie Kirsch
Layout Design: Mark Conrad
Cover Concept: Nick Greenwood

www.summerbridgeactivities.com

Printed in the USA • All rights reserved.                    ISBN: 978-1-60022-152-1

# TABLE OF CONTENTS

# FORMULAS

Solving math problems can be easy if you know some common mathematical formulas. Study the formulas and use this page as a reference as you work through this book.

## Abbreviations

pi = π = 3.14     r = radius        w = width        d = diameter

l = length         h = height      b = base

## Area

of a circle: $\pi r^2$                of a rectangle: lw

of a square: $w^2$             of a triangle: $\frac{1}{2}$(bh)

## Surface Area

of a cylinder: $2\pi(r^2 + rh)$, or $2(\pi r^2) + 2(\pi rh)$

of a cube: $6w^2$

of a sphere: $4\pi r^2$

of a rectangular prism: 2(ab + ac + bc); a, b, and c are the lengths of the 3 sides

## Volume

of a cube: $w^3$              of a cone: $\frac{1}{3} \pi r^2 h$

of a cylinder: $\pi r^2 h$        of a pyramid: $\frac{1}{3}$bh

of a rectangular prism: lwh

## Perimeter

of a circle: πd or 2πr

of a square: 4w

of a rectangle: 2(a + b)

of a triangle: a + b + c

---

**3**

# ASSESSMENT TEST

Circle the number of the correct answer for each question.

**A.** Which of the following products is less than 3 but greater than 0?

   **I.** 3 times 0
   **2.** 3 times a positive whole number
   **3.** 3 times a positive fraction that is less than 1
   **4.** 3 times a negative mixed number

**B.** Which angle has the same measure as ∠CDE?

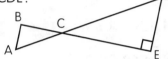

   **I.** ∠ABC           **2.** ∠BCA
   **3.** ∠BAC           **4.** ∠DCE

**C.** What is the rule for the sequence of numbers below?

3, 5, 9, 17, 33 . . .

   **I.** Square the number; then subtract 4.
   **2.** Triple the number; then subtract 4.
   **3.** Double the number; then subtract 1.
   **4.** Quadruple the number; then subtract 7.

**D.** Pack-and-Ship sells boxes to
customers who bring items to the
store to mail and need a shipping
carton. One of their most popular
boxes is the Footer, which has a
volume of 1 cubic foot. The dimensions
are shown at right. The next size up
is the Doubler, which has double the
size of each dimension of the smaller box. What is the volume of the
Doubler?

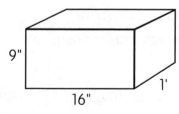

   **I.** 2 cubic feet           **2.** 4 cubic feet
   **3.** 6 cubic feet           **4.** 8 cubic feet

           Math • RB-904064

**E.** Which problem can be solved with this formula?   $70 + 0.15n = 220$

   **I.** The cost of attending a fund-raising dinner is $70.00 per person with the first 15 people admitted free.

   **2.** Buy-the-Week Rental Car advertises that $70.00 will "buy" you a car for a week, but it also charges $0.15 per mile driven. How many miles can a renter get for $220.00?

   **3.** A fast food franchise offers a small soda for $0.70. Refills cost $0.15 each. How many refills can a person get for $220.00?

   **4.** An electrician charges a base fee of $70.00 for each house call he makes. He then charges $15.00 per hour up to a total of $220.00. After that, the homeowner pays $10.00 per hour.

**F.** What is the probability of rolling a total of 7 with a pair of dice?

   **I.** 1:6           **2.** 1:5

   **3.** 6:1           **4.** 5:1

**G.** Which choice below has the integers placed in ascending order?

   **I.** 2, 0, -2, -5, -8        **2.** -3, -6, -9, -12, -15

   **3.** -4, -2, 0, 1, 5         **4.** 0, -1, -2, -3, -4

**H.** Which of these letters of the alphabet has more than one line of symmetry?

   **I.** B           **2.** H

   **3.** E           **4.** K

**I.** Maggie polled the members of her class on whether they preferred pizza or tacos for lunch on Fridays. Thirteen said they preferred pizza, 9 said they preferred tacos, 5 liked both pizza and tacos, and 3 didn't care for either one. In the Venn diagram below, what number should replace the X in the diagram?

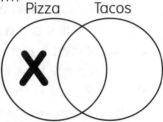

**1.** 3                    **2.** 4

**3.** 5                    **4.** 8

**J.** Faith's father showed her "where the money goes" by sharing the Robinson family budget with her. Which of the following statements is false?

**1.** Food was the most costly expense in the family's budget.
**2.** Clothing and insurance together accounted for more than one fourth of the budget.
**3.** Taxes, utilities and housing costs account for half of the budget.
**4.** Miscellaneous accounted for only $\frac{1}{20}$ of the budget.

**K.** In Saddlebrooke, 8,250 of the homeowners living there do not owe any money on their homes. There are 29,500 homeowners living in Saddlebrooke. What percentage of homeowners still owe money on their homes? (Round to the closest whole percent.)

**1.** 18%                    **2.** 28%

**3.** 72%                    **4.** 82%

Math • RB-904064

Check answers using the answer key provided (page 76). Match those problems with incorrect answers to the sections below. To ensure extra practice in problem areas, refer to the pages listed under each section.

## Number and Operations
Questions: A, C, G, and K
Review Pages: 8, 14, 15, 16, 18, 19, 23, 24, 25, 27, 28, 36, 39, 41, 42, 45, 48, 51, 55, 59, 64, 70, 74

## Geometry
Questions: B, D, H, and I
Review Pages: 9, 13, 21, 25, 26, 33, 34, 35, 37, 38, 40, 43, 44, 46, 52, 53, 58, 60, 66, 72

## Measurement
Question: D
Review Pages: 10, 12, 18, 33, 34, 35, 44, 46, 48, 50, 54, 59, 60, 61, 65, 66, 73

## Data Analysis
Questions: I and J
Review Pages: 22, 30, 31, 32, 42, 50, 52, 62, 63, 69, 71, 74

## Algebra
Questions: C and E
Review Pages: 15, 17, 20, 22, 29, 49, 56, 57

## Probability
Question: F
Review Pages: 11, 47, 67, 68, 75

Math • RB-904064

A *prime number* is a number whose only factors are 1 and the number itself. The number 1 is not a prime number. Your task is to identify all of the numbers from 2 to 100 that are prime numbers. Follow these instructions, and you will find them easily.

- Circle number 2. Then, cross out all of the multiples of 2.
- Circle number 3. Then, cross out all of the multiples of 3.
- Circle number 5. Then, cross out all of the multiples of 5.
- Circle number 7. Then, cross out all of the multiples of 7.
- Circle the remaining numbers that have not been crossed out. All of the circled numbers are prime numbers.

|    | 2  | 3  | 4  | 5  | 6  | 7  | 8  | 9  | 10  |
|----|----|----|----|----|----|----|----|----|-----|
| 11 | 12 | 13 | 14 | 15 | 16 | 17 | 18 | 19 | 20  |
| 21 | 22 | 23 | 24 | 25 | 26 | 27 | 28 | 29 | 30  |
| 31 | 32 | 33 | 34 | 35 | 36 | 37 | 38 | 39 | 40  |
| 41 | 42 | 43 | 44 | 45 | 46 | 47 | 48 | 49 | 50  |
| 51 | 52 | 53 | 54 | 55 | 56 | 57 | 58 | 59 | 60  |
| 61 | 62 | 63 | 64 | 65 | 66 | 67 | 68 | 69 | 70  |
| 71 | 72 | 73 | 74 | 75 | 76 | 77 | 78 | 79 | 80  |
| 81 | 82 | 83 | 84 | 85 | 86 | 87 | 88 | 89 | 90  |
| 91 | 92 | 93 | 94 | 95 | 96 | 97 | 98 | 99 | 100 |

How many prime numbers are there that are less than 100?_____

© Rainbow Bridge Publishing

Math • RB-904064

*Geometry*

Each row below contains tiles with letters that combine to spell a 10-letter word. Unscramble the letters and change their positions to spell the word. Then, write the word in the line.

A. _____    HB | OT | SH | OT | RU

B. _____    WB | RA | RY | ER | ST

C. _____    EB | RD | SC | OA | OR

D. _____    RE | TI | EA | CR | ON

E. _____    OT | BO | RY | RA | LA

F. _____    LI | TF | DE | UL | GH

Describe a pattern in the arrangement of the above words.

_____

_____

_____

_____

_____

Math • RB-904064

# PICTURE THIS!

Find the area of each picture frame below. To do this, find the area of each frame's outside dimensions. Then, subtract the image area that the photo occupies. Look for a pattern between the area of the frames and the widths.

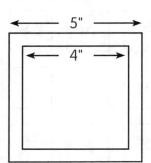
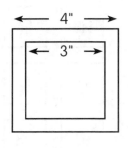
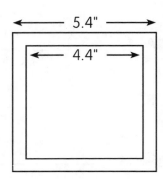

**A.** _____  **B.** _____  **C.** _____

**D.** What pattern did you discover?_____

_____

_____

Find the area of each picture frame.

**E.** Outside measurement: 6.5"; Inside measurement: 5.5" _____

**F.** Outside measurement: 8"; Inside measurement: 7" _____

**G.** Outside measurement: 10"; Inside measurement: 9"_____

**H.** What conclusions can you draw? _____

_____

_____

*Probability*

*Probability* is the ratio of favorable outcomes of an event happening to the total number of possible outcomes. For example, if you roll a die, the odds of rolling a 3 are 1:6. Since there are six numbers on the cube, you have a 1 in 6 chance of winning or 1 favorable chance (rolling a 3) against 6 possible outcomes (rolling a 1, 2, 3, 4, 5, or 6).

You can express the odds either as the odds against an event happening (5:6 in the case of the odds against rolling a 3) or as the odds of an event actually happening (1:6 in the case of the odds that you will roll a 3). You must always look at the way the statement is presented to determine which way to express the odds.

Look at each situation below and write the odds of the event successfully happening.

**A.** There are 11 marbles in a bag. Four are red, 3 are blue, 3 are green, and 1 is clear. What are the odds that you will draw either a blue or a clear marble? _____

What are the odds that the marble will not be green? _____

**B.** What are the odds of rolling an even number on a six-sided die?

_____

**C.** A pizza has 9 slices. Two of the slices have pepperoni on them. What are the odds of choosing a slice that does not have pepperoni on it? _____

**D.** There are 4 queens and 4 aces in a standard deck of 52 playing cards. What are the odds of choosing a queen or an ace from a standard deck of cards? _____

Look at the map below showing a short section of Highway 101. Silver Springs is 4 miles from Catalina and 30 miles from Marana. Apache Junction is $\frac{2}{3}$ of the distance between Silver Springs and Marana.

**A.** How far is it from Catalina to Apache Junction?
(Measure from dot to dot.) _____

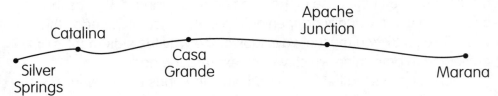

Bear Canyon is located outside the town of Apache Junction. Use the map to answer questions **B**, **C**, and **D**. (Measure from dot to dot.)
**1" = 500 yards.**

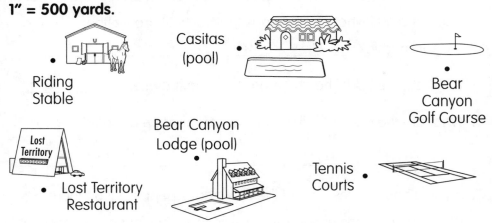

**B.** How far is it from the Bear Canyon Lodge to the golf course? _____

**C.** For someone staying in one of the casitas, how far is it to the Lost Territory Restaurant?_____

**D.** How far would someone staying in a casita travel to play tennis, return to his room to change and go for a swim, and go to the riding stable for a horseback ride? _____

Look carefully at the solid shown below. (The front view is shown.)

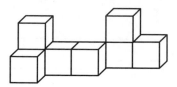

**A.** Which of the following represents the view of the solid from the top?

1.
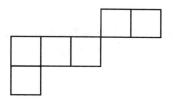

2.
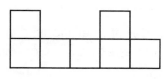

3.
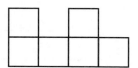

4.

**B.** Which is the view from the front?_____

**C.** Look at the stack of 9 cubes below and draw how the stack looks from a top view.

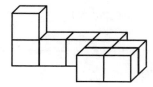

# ORDER OF OPERATIONS

In descending order, list the four rules that apply to the order of operations.

_____

_____

_____

_____

Use the order of operations to simplify each math expression. Write a number expression for each phrase below. Then, evaluate the expression.

**A.** $28 \div 7 + 10 =$ _____

**B.** $6 \times 2 + 6 \times 3 =$ _____

**C.** $40 - 3 \times 4 + 5 =$ _____

**D.** $(10 - 7) \times 3 - 10 =$ _____

**E.** $9 + 6 - 12 + 8 =$ _____

**F.** $(7 + 2) \div (7 - 4) =$ _____

**G.** $-6 \times 3 \times 6 \times -3 =$ _____

**H.** $42 \times 5 - 22 =$ _____

**I.** $23 - 5 =$ _____

**J.** $14 \div 7 - 5 =$ _____

**K.** $8 - 1 \times 4 \div 2 =$ _____

**L.** $18 \times (3 + 1) \div 3 =$ _____

**M.** 15 times 10 times 2 divided by 60 _____

**N.** 15 plus 7 times 5 _____

**O.** 14.5 minus 28.5 divided by 5 _____

**P.** 2.4 times 2 minus 5.2 _____

**Q.** The quantity 8 minus 5 times 6 minus 12 _____

**R.** The quantity 14 minus 5 divided by the quantity 9 minus 6

_____

Math • RB-904064

*Algebra, Number and Operations*

Read each set of clues below to determine the pair of numbers that meet the criteria. Some answers will be negative numbers.

**A.** Their sum is 10. Their product is 25. Dividing the two numbers results in a quotient of 1. Their difference is 0. What are the two numbers?

_____

**B.** Their sum is 6. Their difference is 4. Multiplying them together leads to a product of 5. Dividing the larger by the smaller results in a quotient of 5. What are the two numbers? _____

**C.** Their product is 6. Their difference is 1. Their sum is -5. Dividing the smaller by the larger yields a quotient of 1.5. What are the two numbers?_____

**D.** Their sum is 21. Their difference is 15. Their product is 54. The quotient is 6 when the larger is divided by the smaller. What are the two numbers?_____

**E.** Their sum is 16. Their product is 192. Their quotient is either -3 or -0.333. What are the two numbers? _____

**F.** Their sum is –3. Their product is –4. Their difference is 5. What are the two numbers? _____

**G.** Their sum is 0. Their product is 36. Their difference is 12. Their quotient is 1. What are the two numbers?_____

**H.** The difference between their sum and their product is 15. Their product is 27. What are the two numbers?_____

Math • RB-904064

# WHAT IS THAT NUMBER?

Write the answer for each question.

**A.** It is a prime number between 100 and 120. The sum of the digits equals 8. The number is _____.

**B.** It is a composite number between 20 and 30. The sum of the digits equals 9. The number is_____.

**C.** It is a prime number between 60 and 100. The sum of the digits equals 11. The number is _____.

**D.** It is a multiple of 7. The number is less than 100. The sum of the digits equals 12. The number is_____.

**E.** It is a composite number between 10 and 30. The number is even. The sum of the digits equals 8. The number is_____.

**F.** It is a composite number between 80 and 90. The number is even. The sum of the digits equals 16. The number is _____.

**G.** It is a prime number between 40 and 50. The number is 2 greater than another prime number. The number is _____.

**H.** It is an even number between 10 and 40. The number is a multiple of 12. The sum of the digits is 9. The number is _____.

**I.** It is a multiple of 11 and an odd number. The number is between 100 and 150. The sum of the digits equals 4. The number is _____.

**J.** It is a prime number. The number is 2 more than another prime number and between 120 and 140. The sum of the digits equals 13. The number is_____.

*Algebra*

Look at each row to determine the pattern that is presented. Then, draw the missing symbol or symbols that will make the pattern complete in the space provided.

**A.**

**B.**

**C.**

**D.**

**E.** ◺◹◺◺◹__◹◺◺◹◺__◹

**F.** ⊕⊗⊛✳⊕__⊛__⊕

 Math • RB-904064

For a teeter-totter to balance, the weight at one end multiplied by the weight's distance from the fulcrum must equal the weight at the other end multiplied by that weight's distance from the fulcrum.

**A.** Raul weighs 110 pounds and sits 48" from the center of the teeter-totter. Randy, his seesaw partner, weighs 88 pounds. How far should he sit from the center to balance the teeter-totter?

_____

**B.** Cam, who weighs 102 pounds, has his little sister Kari with him. She weighs only 30 pounds. Cam's friend Jake weighs 115.5 pounds. If Jake sits 48" from the center, where should Cam and Kari sit to balance the teeter-totter?

_____

**C.** Lillie weighs 104 pounds and sits 45" from the fulcrum. Logan does not want anyone to know his weight, but he sits only $\frac{4}{5}$ of the distance Lillie is positioned from the fulcrum. How much does Logan weigh?

_____

**D.** Several students want to use the teeter-totter at the same time. They decide to put two people on each end. Leah weighs 94 pounds, and her buddy Rachel weighs 98 pounds. How far should they sit from the center if Mandy (82 pounds) and Mindy (86 pounds) sit 48" from the center? (Round your answer to the closest inch.)

_____

*Number and Operations*

Look at the letters displayed on a telephone keypad.

Use the keypad to decode the names of these locations:

**A.** 423-5263 _____

**B.** 437-6269 _____

**C.** 364-5263 _____

**D.** 526-2422 _____

Sometimes businesses use keypads to spell phone numbers they want their customers to remember. Then, if customers forget the number, they can spell out the business's name. See if you can crack the code for each business below.

**E.** Local glass repair service providing on-site service for broken glass
1-800-464-5277 _____

**F.** Accounting firm specializing in income tax preparation
1-800-829-4357 _____

Math • RB-904064

# RATIO RUNDOWN

Use the piano keyboard below to answer questions **A**, **B**, and **C**.

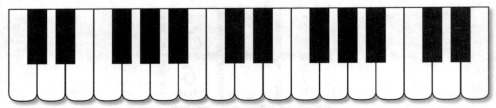

**A.** What is the ratio of white keys to black keys on the keyboard? _____

**B.** What is the ratio of black keys to the total number of keys? _____

**C.** What is the ratio of white keys to the total number of keys? _____

Use the table below to answer questions **D**, **E**, and **F**.

## Seafood Medley

|            | Apprentice | Ship's Mate | First Mate | Captain's Choice |
|------------|:----------:|:-----------:|:----------:|:----------------:|
| White Fish | 3          | 4.5         | 6          | 9                |
| Shrimp     | 2          | 3           | 4          | 6                |
| Lobster    | 1          | 1.5         | 2          | 3                |

**D.** What is the ratio of lobster pieces to shrimp pieces in each dish in the Seafood Medley? _____

**E.** What is the ratio of white fish pieces to the number of pieces in the entire Captain's Choice dish? _____

**F.** Which of the following expresses the ratio of shrimp pieces to white fish pieces in the Seafood Medley? Circle your choice.

2 to 3 $\qquad$ $\frac{2}{3}$ $\qquad$ 2:3 $\qquad$ all three choices

*Geometry*

Answer the questions.

**A.** Gretchen has decided to plant a vegetable garden. She plans to grow three 20' rows of carrots. Planting instructions tell her to plant the seeds 2" apart. How many seeds does she need for her carrot patch?

_____

**B.** Gretchen also wants tomatoes in her garden, but she has decided to buy small tomato plants rather than grow the tomatoes from seeds. She will plant the tomatoes 36" apart to give them plenty of room. If she wants to plant 20 plants, how many square feet should she allow in her garden for her tomato plants? **Hint:** A rough diagram is sometimes useful in solving this kind of problem.

_____

**C.** After Gretchen finished planting vegetables, she had space left in her garden. Gretchen decided to plant herbs in the remaining space. After measuring her space, she bought 15 plants and planted them 18" apart. How many square feet of space did Gretchen have left in her garden before she planted her herbs?

_____

Math • RB-904064

# ANNIE'S NEW PHONE

As a reward for making the honor roll, Annie's parents gave her permission to get her own mobile phone. They asked her to "shop around" for the best deal. She narrowed the field to three possibilities.

Spider Cellular offers a plan for $29.95 that provides 250 "free minutes" per month and then charges $0.40 per minute for each minute after that. Stay-in-Touch Wireless provides a plan with no monthly fee, but charges $0.15 per minute for every minute the phone is used. Finally, Cristini Wireless charges $19.95 per month for the first 100 minutes and $0.20 per minute for each minute after 100.

To figure out the best rate, Annie chose several different usage points and compared plan costs at each point. Use the table below to figure out the costs of the three plans. Include the monthly fees if applicable.

| # of Minutes | 0 | 100 | 200 | 300 |
|---|---|---|---|---|
| Spider Cellular | | | | |
| Stay-in-Touch | | | | |
| Cristini Wireless | | | | |

If Annie uses her phone for 300 minutes a month, which plan would be best for her? Justify your choice using the rates of the various plans you have calculated.

_____

_____

_____

_____

*Number and Operations*

Create number sentences by providing the multipliers that will make the products at the end of each row and bottom of each column correct. Do not use the number 1. Use fractions if necessary.

| | | | | | |
|---|---|---|---|---|---|
| 18 | X | | X | | = 6 |
| X | ■ | X | ■ | X | ■ |
| 6 | X | | X | | = 2 |
| X | ■ | X | ■ | X | ■ |
| | X | 12 | X | | = 18 |
| = 9 | ■ | = 4 | ■ | = 6 | ■ |

Math • RB-904064

# SCHOOL SHOPPING

José and his mother went school shopping. José had saved some money. His mother said she would spend $2.00 for every dollar of his own money that José spent.

Their first stop was to buy a new pair of shoes, José's top priority. Mrs. Garcia gave the cashier José's portion and paid her part of the shoes with a credit card. At the clothing store, José bought a new pair of jeans, four T-shirts, a pair of khaki pants, and a shirt with a collar. José's share was $36.00.

José volunteered to buy their lunch. Mrs. Garcia was delighted with José's generosity and left a $2.00 tip for the waiter. The lunch cost José $13.00. He now had only $16.00 left. His mother agreed to pay for all of his school supplies. So, José spent the rest of his money on a new CD.

José's school supplies cost $26.00. Mrs. Garcia's charges for the day were $148.00.

**A.** How much money did José spend? _____

**B.** If he spent only one-third of the money he saved during the summer, how much did José have left? _____

**C.** If the money he spent school shopping plus the money he had left represented only 40% of the money he made during the summer, how much money did José earn during the summer?

_____

**D.** How much did this school shopping spree cost José and his mother? _____

*Geometry, Number and Operations*

Look at each drawing and decide which estimate of the area shaded comes closest to the correct percent. Circle your answers.

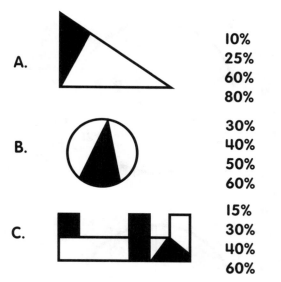

**A.**
10%
25%
60%
80%

**B.**
30%
40%
50%
60%

**C.**
15%
30%
40%
60%

Now, it's time to try it yourself. Shade the indicated portion of each drawing below.

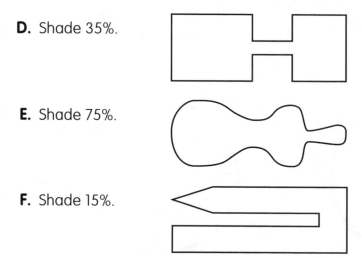

**D.** Shade 35%.

**E.** Shade 75%.

**F.** Shade 15%.

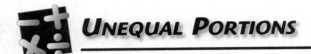

Estimate the portions of each pie in the blanks.

1.

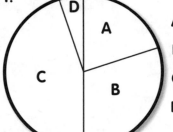

A. ____
B. ____
C. ____
D. ____

2.

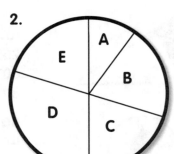

A. ____
B. ____
C. ____
D. ____
E. ____

3.

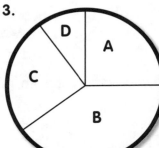

A. ____
B. ____
C. ____
D. ____

4.

A. ____
B. ____
C. ____
D. ____
E. ____

5.

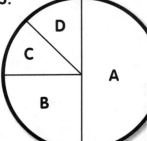

A. ____
B. ____
C. ____
D. ____

6.

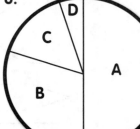

A. ____
B. ____
C. ____
D. ____

    Math • RB-904064

*Number and Operations*

Look at the two numbers in the top line of the first box below. Then, look at the bottom two numbers. Decide how these two sets of numbers were used to arrive at the number in the middle. Do the same for the second box. Use the same pattern to find the number in the middle of the third box.

**A.**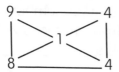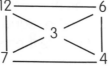

Describe the pattern used in the first two boxes to arrive at the number in the middle. _____

_____

What is the missing number in the middle of the third box? _____

**B.**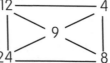

Describe the pattern used in the first two boxes to arrive at the number in the middle. _____

_____

What is the missing number in the middle of the third box? _____

**C.**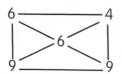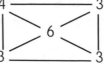

Describe the pattern used in the first two boxes to arrive at the number in the middle. _____

_____

What is the missing number in the middle of the third box? _____

Math • RB-904064

# I'M THINKING OF NUMBERS

Read each clue below and decide which numbers fit each situation.

**A.** Divide the larger by the smaller and the quotient is 3. Their difference is 6. Their sum is 12, and their product is 27. What are the two numbers? _____

**B.** Make the smaller number the numerator and the larger number the denominator. The fraction can be reduced to $\frac{1}{2}$. Their product is 72 and their difference is 6. What are the two numbers? _____

**C.** Make the larger number the divisor and the smaller number the dividend. The quotient becomes 0.75. The difference between the numbers is 1. The product of the two numbers is 12. What are the numbers? _____

**D.** Their difference is 6. Their product is 216. Divide the larger number by the smaller number, and the quotient is 1.5. Their total equals 30. What are the two numbers? _____

**E.** Their difference is 14. Their product is -24. Divide the larger number by the smaller number, and the quotient is -6. Their sum equals 10. What are the two numbers? _____

**F.** Divide the smaller number by the larger number, and the quotient is 2. The difference between the two numbers is 8. Their product is 128. What are the two numbers? _____

**G.** Their total is -6. Their product is 8. Their difference is 2. Dividing the larger number by the smaller number results in a quotient of $\frac{1}{2}$. What are the two numbers? _____

**H.** If you subtract the smaller number from the larger number, the difference is 7. Multiply the two, and the product equals 120. The sum of the two numbers equals 23. What are the two numbers? _____

 Math • RB-904064

*Algebra*

The steps for solving an unknown equation are presented below. Use the given value of x and reverse the operations in the steps to find the original equation.

**Example:** Add 3x to each side.
Add 3 to each side.
Divide each side by 4.
$x = 1$

**Solution:** $4x = 4$
$4x - 3 = 1$
**Equation:** $x - 3 = 1 - 3x$

**A.** Subtract 3x from each side.
Subtract 5 from each side.
Divide each side by 3.
$x = 3$

**Solution:**

**Equation:** _____

**B.** Add 8 to each side.
Divide each side by 3.
$x = 5$

**Solution:**

**Equation:** _____

**C.** Subtract 4 from each side.
Multiply each side by 3.
$x = 15$

**Solution:**

**Equation:** _____

Math • RB-904064

Eleven members of Troop #39 and their leader went to Camp Saukenauk for their end-of-summer camping and canoe trip.

Below is a drawing of their positions around the campfire after dinner. Each boy cooked his own food and made whatever he wanted to eat. On the diagram, show where the leader sat and list the food eaten by each camper at each place.

1. Three boys made veggie burgers. They later sat next to each other.
2. One boy made chili and later sat to the left of the camp leader.
3. Two boys cooked hot dogs. Each hot dog eater sat between two hamburger eaters during the campfire.
4. The campfire was directly north of the leader's seat.
5. Two boys warmed up precooked chicken fingers and later sat next to each other.
6. One of the veggie burger eaters sat to the left of the boy who fixed chili.
7. One of the boys who had chicken fingers had a veggie burger eater sitting to his right.

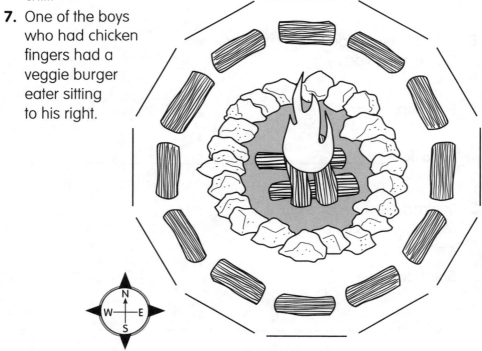

Math • RB-904064

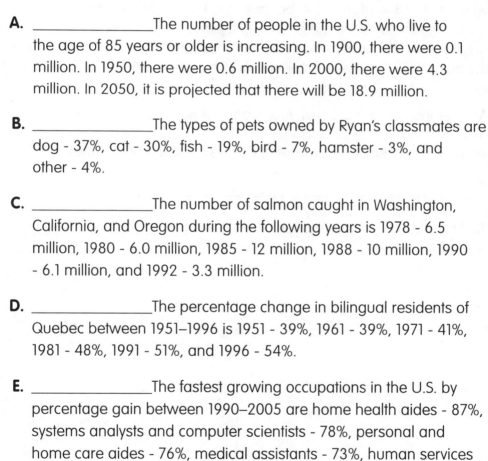

# THE BEST GRAPH

*Data Analysis*

After you have collected data, the next step is to determine how to present that data so that it makes sense and has meaning for others. Indicate whether you would choose a bar graph, a line graph, or a circle graph to present each set of data.

**A.** _____The number of people in the U.S. who live to the age of 85 years or older is increasing. In 1900, there were 0.1 million. In 1950, there were 0.6 million. In 2000, there were 4.3 million. In 2050, it is projected that there will be 18.9 million.

**B.** _____The types of pets owned by Ryan's classmates are dog - 37%, cat - 30%, fish - 19%, bird - 7%, hamster - 3%, and other - 4%.

**C.** _____The number of salmon caught in Washington, California, and Oregon during the following years is 1978 - 6.5 million, 1980 - 6.0 million, 1985 - 12 million, 1988 - 10 million, 1990 - 6.1 million, and 1992 - 3.3 million.

**D.** _____The percentage change in bilingual residents of Quebec between 1951–1996 is 1951 - 39%, 1961 - 39%, 1971 - 41%, 1981 - 48%, 1991 - 51%, and 1996 - 54%.

**E.** _____The fastest growing occupations in the U.S. by percentage gain between 1990–2005 are home health aides - 87%, systems analysts and computer scientists - 78%, personal and home care aides - 76%, medical assistants - 73%, human services workers - 71%, and radiology technicians - 70%.

Math • RB-904064

# ANNUAL SALES MEETING

Local employees of the Hartman Insurance Company gathered in early February for their annual sales strategy meeting in downtown Chicago, Illinois. Some arrived by car. Eleven took the commuter train. Those who arrived by car were friends who carpooled from an area where they all lived. The number averaged 4 people per car.

During the week, some people who arrived by train became acquainted with others who lived near them. When they left, only 8 rode the train. The average number traveling in cars was 4.5 people per car.

Answer the questions. Show your work in the space below.

**A.** How many employees were in the group attending the meeting?

_____

**B.** How many cars were driven to the meeting?_____

*Measurement, Geometry*

Conover Cans, Inc. makes cans for many different companies. The company's success rests on its ability to create precisely the kind of container best suited to each customer's needs.

Conover currently makes a cylindrical can that is 5" high with a circular base that has a radius of 2" for one of their customers. A customer now wants Conover to create a prototype of a can that is 2" high with a circular base that has a radius of 5".

**A.** Find the volume of the cylindrical can currently in use. Round to the nearest cubic inch. Use 3.14 for the value of pi.

_____

**B.** Find the volume of the prototype can. Round to the nearest cubic inch. Use 3.14 for the value of pi.

_____

**C.** How tall would the current can need to be to have approximately the same volume as the prototype can? Round your answer to the nearest half inch. _____

**D.** What size shipping carton would you suggest if the customer wants to ship 24 of the new containers in each case?_____

Explain your reasons for the size of shipping carton you suggest.

_____

_____

_____

© Rainbow Bridge Publishing     Math • RB-904064

# COMPARING SURFACE AREAS

The *surface area* of a cylinder is the sum of the lateral surface plus the area of the two bases. The formula is:

Surface area = $2\pi rh + 2\pi r^2$

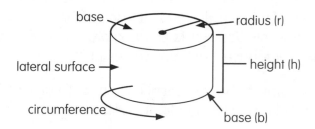

Answer the questions. Use the space below to show your work.

**A.** If the radius of a can is 8 cm and the height of the can is 22 cm, what is the surface area of the can?

_____

**B.** Brad is making building blocks for his younger brother, Daniel. He plans to cut 4" sections from five 36" dowels that have a 3" diameter. How many cylindrical blocks can Brad make? _____

**C.** After sanding the edges, Brad decides to paint the cylinders with nontoxic paint. He has several small containers of paint that will each cover 180 square inches. How many containers of paint does Brad need to paint all of the cylindrical blocks he made for his brother?_____

*Geometry, Measurement*

This chart shows the population figures for the 10 largest U.S. cities as of July 1, 2002, and April 1, 2000. Using the chart below, calculate the percentage change experienced by each city. Record your calculation in the column headed "% Change." Round the percentage change to the nearest tenth of a percent.

**A.** Which city had the greatest percentage increase in population?

_____

**B.** Which city experienced the greatest decrease in population?

_____

| Rank | City | July 1, 2002 | April 1, 2000 | % Change |
|------|------|--------------|---------------|----------|
| 1 | New York, NY | 8,084,316 | 8,008,038 | |
| 2 | Los Angeles, CA | 3,798,981 | 3,694,742 | |
| 3 | Chicago, IL | 2,886,251 | 2,896,047 | |
| 4 | Houston, TX | 2,009,834 | 1,953,633 | |
| 5 | Philadelphia, PA | 1,492,231 | 1,517,550 | |
| 6 | Phoenix, AZ | 1,371,190 | 1,321,190 | |
| 7 | San Diego, CA | 1,259,532 | 1,223,416 | |
| 8 | Dallas, TX | 1,211,467 | 1,188,589 | |
| 9 | San Antonio, TX | 1,194,222 | 1,151,268 | |
| 10 | Detroit, MI | 925,051 | 951,270 | |

© Rainbow Bridge Publishing

Math • RB-904064

For each statement, think of something in the real world you could estimate to fit the description.

**Example:** It's over 100 years old. The answer could be a tree.

1. It weighs about one pound. _____
2. It happens only once a year. _____
3. It is over 50' tall! _____
4. It is over a thousand miles from here. _____
5. It is the oldest thing I've ever touched. _____
6. It can hold five gallons. _____
7. It costs about $100,000.00. _____
8. Its value is priceless! _____
9. It happens once every hour. _____
10. It is somewhere between good and bad. _____
11. It could hold a million of them! _____
12. I spend at least 3 hours a day doing it! _____
13. It can hold up to 200 pounds. _____
14. It should last only about a second. _____
15. The area is about 3,500 square feet. _____
16. There are only about 5,000 of them. _____
17. There must be a million lights there! _____
18. It is not worth saving. _____
19. Everyone should own at least one. _____
20. There are only two of them in this entire school! _____
21. That is worth its weight in gold! _____
22. A half-hour should be plenty of time to do this. _____
23. It is the biggest thing I have ever seen! _____
24. I just can't sit still that long! _____

Math • RB-904064

*Geometry*

Hanna Housewright has been around horses all of her life. In her spare time, she trains horses to earn extra money. Below is a drawing of the circular horse arena she uses to train the horses. The arena covers 7,800 square feet. Use the drawing to answer questions **A** and **B**.

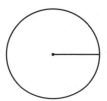

**A.** The training arena covers 7,800 square feet. How long must Hanna's rope be if she stands in the center and guides the horse in a circle around the perimeter of the arena? **Hint:** This means she is trying to find the radius of her circular arena. Use 3.14 for the value of pi.

_____

**B.** Hanna's dad wants to build a wooden fence around the arena. The 6' high fencing he has in mind costs $8.50 per linear foot. If he installs the fence himself, how much will he pay for the cost of the fence? **Hint:** Remember that the formula for finding the perimeter of a circle is C = pi x d.

_____

**C.** The horse barn on the Housewright farm measures 70' x 40'. There is an aisle down the middle of the barn that is 70' long and 16' wide for storing food, water, and saddles. If each stall is 14' long and 12' wide, how many stalls does Hanna have in the barn? **Hint:** Draw a simple diagram to help you visualize the layout of Hanna's barn.

_____

Math • RB-904064

# THE PYTHAGOREAN TRIPLE

*Geometry*

Pythagoras was a famous Greek mathematician and philosopher who was interested in the concept of number, the concept of a triangle, and the abstract idea of a proof.

Nicknamed "the father of numbers," Pythagoras is best remembered for being the first to prove that in a right triangle the square of the *hypotenuse* (the long side of the triangle opposite the right angle) is equal to the sum of the squares of the other two sides of the triangle. This equation is known as the Pythagorean theorem.

Look at the triangle at the right.

Note the following relationship:

$$a^2 + b^2 = c^2$$

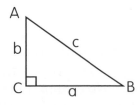

Any three positive numbers that satisfy the relationship can be the lengths of the sides of right triangles. The set of three numbers is known as a *Pythagorean Triple*.

Find the length of the missing side of each right triangle below by using the Pythagorean theorem.

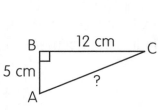

**A.** _____

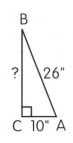

**B.** _____

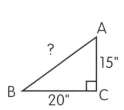

**C.** _____

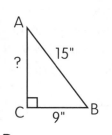

**D.** _____

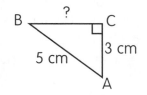

**E.** _____

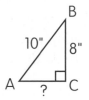

**F.** _____

© Rainbow Bridge Publishing                                    Math • RB-904064

*Number and Operations*

Study the numbers in each square below and fill in the missing numbers.

**A.**

|  |  |  | 65 |  |  |
|---|---|---|---|---|---|
|  |  |  |  |  |  |
|  | 155 |  |  |  |  |
| 95 |  | 165 |  |  | 40 |
|  |  |  |  | 120 |  |
|  | 10 |  | 20 |  |  |

What pattern do you see in the arrangement of numbers in each section?

_____

**B.**

| 10 |  |  |  |  | 60 |
|---|---|---|---|---|---|
|  | 22 |  |  | 52 |  |
|  |  | 34 |  |  |  |
| 16 |  |  |  |  |  |
|  |  | 38 |  |  |  |
|  |  |  | 50 |  |  |

What pattern did you discover in this square? _____

_____

Math • RB-904064

Study the diagram below. Then, answer questions **A–E**.

**A.** What is the relationship between lines A and B?_____

**B.** What is the relationship between lines C and B?_____

**C.** What kind of angle is ∠x? _____

_____

**D.** What kind of angle is ∠y? _____

_____

**E.** What kind of angle is ∠z? _____

_____

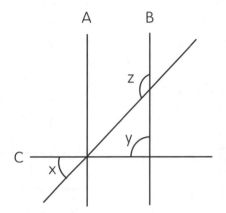

For questions **F–J**, draw a diagram showing the following lines:

    Lines A, B, and C are parallel to each other.

    Line D is perpendicular to line A.

Read each statement. Circle **T** for true or **F** for false to indicate whether the statement accurately describes lines A, B, C, and D.

**F.**   T   F   Line A intersects Line B at a right angle.

**G.**   T   F   Line B is parallel to Line D.

**H.**   T   F   Line C is perpendicular to Line A.

**I.**   T   F   Line D intersects Line C at a right angle.

**J.**   T   F   Line C forms a right angle at the point where it intersects Line A.

Math • RB-904064

*Number and Operations*

The sum of 10 two-digit numbers is less than 200. Read each of the following statements and decide whether the statement is true, possibly true, or false. Write your answers on the lines.

**A.** _____Each number must be less than 10.

**B.** _____If 8 of the numbers are as small as they could be, then the other 2 numbers must be at least 59 each.

**C.** _____If 9 of the numbers are greater than 10, the other number must be at least 89.

**D.** _____If all 10 numbers are different, then their sum must be greater than or equal to 190.

**E.** _____If 2 of the numbers are less than 60 each, then none of the other numbers can be more than 40.

**F.** _____If 6 of the numbers are less than 20, then the other 4 must at least be 20 each.

**G.** _____If 7 of the numbers add up to 77, then none of the remaining 3 numbers can be larger than 41.

**H.** _____If 3 of the numbers total 100, then each of the remaining 7 numbers can be larger than 12.

**I.** _____If 8 of the numbers are at least 20 each, then neither of the remaining 2 numbers can be greater than 29.

**J.** _____If 2 of the numbers add up to 27, then at least 1 of the remaining numbers must be greater than 21.

© Rainbow Bridge Publishing
Math • RB-904064

*Data Analysis, Number and Operations*

Below is the population data collected on the 10 fastest-growing cities in the United States with populations over 100,000. The data is based on population figures as of July 1, 2002, and April 1, 2000.

Use the data to rank which cities are growing the fastest. Base your ranking on the percentage increase in population.

| Rank | City | July 1, 2002 | April 1, 2000 | % Increase |
|---|---|---|---|---|
| | Chula Vista, CA | 193,919 | 173,566 | |
| | Chandler, AZ | 202,016 | 173,566 | |
| | North Las Vegas, NV | 135,902 | 115,488 | |
| | Joliet, IL | 118,423 | 106,334 | |
| | Gilbert, AZ | 135,005 | 109,920 | |
| | Fontana, CA | 143,607 | 128,938 | |
| | Henderson, NV | 206,016 | 175,750 | |
| | Peoria, AZ | 123,239 | 108,685 | |
| | Rancho Cucamonga, CA | 193,919 | 173,566 | |
| | Irvine, CA | 162,122 | 143,072 | |

What conclusions can you draw from this data? _____

_____

_____

_____

_____

_____

Math • RB-904064

*Geometry*

A *coordinate grid* is a two-dimensional system in which the coordinates of a point are its distances from two perpendicular lines called *axes*.

**A.** The horizontal axis is called the_____.

**B.** The vertical axis is called the _____.

**C.** The point where the horizontal and vertical axes meet is called the

_____.

Use the diagram below to answer questions D, E, F, and G.

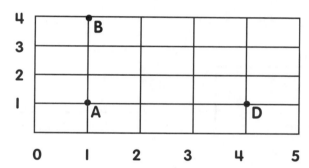

**D.** To complete the diagram as a rectangle, where should the coordinates for Point C be located?_____

Draw this point and label it C.

**E.** What is the distance between Point A and Point D?_____

**F.** If you connected Point C with Point A, Point A with Point B, and Point B with Point C, what kind of triangle would you create? Circle your choice below.

right triangle          equilateral triangle          isosceles triangle

**G.** What kind of triangle would you have if you connected Points C, A, and D?

equilateral triangle     obtuse triangle          scalene triangle

Math • RB-904064

The Lofton family just bought a new ranch-style home near the top of a mountain. The house has a small loft with skylights that extend out over the living room. They decided the loft would be a great place to mount a telescope and observe the beauty of the nighttime sky. There are 11 steps leading to the loft.

Mr. Lofton wants to know how much it will cost to carpet the steps. He knows he must first determine the area of the steps. Look at the diagram below. Find out how many square inches there are in the steps to be carpeted.

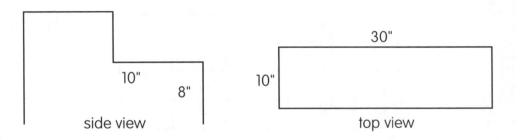

10"     8"
side view

30"
10"
top view

**A.** Area in square inches to be carpeted: _____

**B.** Area of steps in square feet: _____

**C.** The carpet the Loftons have chosen costs $12.75 per square foot. How much will the carpet cost the Loftons? _____

**D.** Mr. Lofton hired Larry Allen to install the carpet at a cost of $3.50 per square foot. How much will the Loftons pay to get their new carpet installed?_____

**E.** What will be the total cost of the Loftons' carpeting project?

_____

# MATTERS OF PROPORTION

*Number and Operations*

Solve each problem below by setting it up as a ratio and proportion problem.

**A.** A popular newspaper costs $2.00 per week for home delivery. The paper is delivered each of the five days through the week, but not on weekends. At this rate, what will a six-month subscription cost per day?

_____

**B.** Sliced swiss cheese in the deli sells for $8.00 per pound. How much will it cost for 6 ounces?_____

**C.** Evan bought an eight-pack of lightbulbs for $5.00 from a local service organization. He thought it was a good deal and decided to compare it with prices in a local discount store. He saw a package of 20 bulbs. What should they cost him if they compare with his earlier purchase?

_____

**D.** Goldfish are selling at Pets-4-U on a weekend special of 3 for $1.00. What will 3 dozen cost? _____

**E.** Will's batting average through the years has been to get 36 hits for every 100 times he batted. How many hits can Will expect to hit this year if he bats 225 times and continues at his same pace?

_____

Math • RB-904064

*Geometry, Measurement*

Decide whether you think each statement is reasonable. If you think the numbers used sound true, write "yes." If you do not think the statement makes sense, write "no."

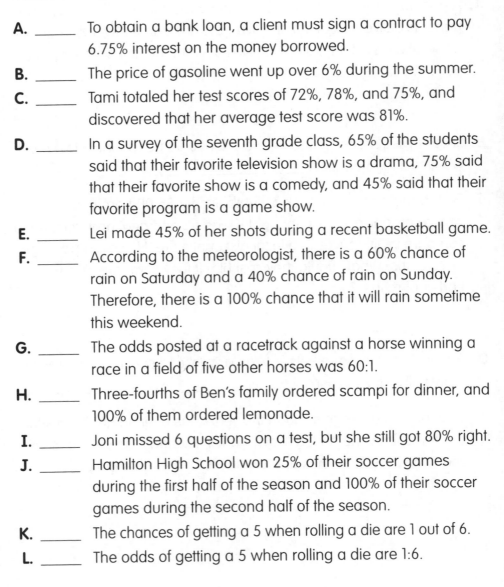

**A.** _____ To obtain a bank loan, a client must sign a contract to pay 6.75% interest on the money borrowed.

**B.** _____ The price of gasoline went up over 6% during the summer.

**C.** _____ Tami totaled her test scores of 72%, 78%, and 75%, and discovered that her average test score was 81%.

**D.** _____ In a survey of the seventh grade class, 65% of the students said that their favorite television show is a drama, 75% said that their favorite show is a comedy, and 45% said that their favorite program is a game show.

**E.** _____ Lei made 45% of her shots during a recent basketball game.

**F.** _____ According to the meteorologist, there is a 60% chance of rain on Saturday and a 40% chance of rain on Sunday. Therefore, there is a 100% chance that it will rain sometime this weekend.

**G.** _____ The odds posted at a racetrack against a horse winning a race in a field of five other horses was 60:1.

**H.** _____ Three-fourths of Ben's family ordered scampi for dinner, and 100% of them ordered lemonade.

**I.** _____ Joni missed 6 questions on a test, but she still got 80% right.

**J.** _____ Hamilton High School won 25% of their soccer games during the first half of the season and 100% of their soccer games during the second half of the season.

**K.** _____ The chances of getting a 5 when rolling a die are 1 out of 6.

**L.** _____ The odds of getting a 5 when rolling a die are 1:6.

Math • RB-904064

*Probability*

Shannon and Emmy are playing a game with a spinner mounted on a circular board. The board is divided into 9 equal sections labeled 1–9. Use the spinner below to answer the questions A-C.

**A.** What chance does Shannon have of landing the spinner on a 5? _____

**B.** What chance does Emmy have of landing on an even number?

_____

**C.** Shannon says that she has a better chance of landing on an odd number than on an even one. How much better are those chances?

_____

**D.** If Emmy rolls a die, what are the chances that she will not get a 5?

_____

**E.** Shannon rolls a die that lands on 3. What are Emmy's chances of rolling a higher number than Shannon?_____

**F.** Emmy rolls the die, and it lands on the 6. If she rolls the die again, what are her chances of rolling another 6? _____

**G.** If the girls roll a pair of dice, what chance does Shannon have of both dice landing on 6?_____

Find the volumes of the objects. **Hint:** Both cones and pyramids have one base and one vertex.

**A.** Find the volume of the cone. Use $\frac{22}{7}$ for pi.

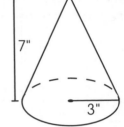

_____

**B.** Find the volume of the pyramid.

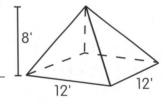

_____

**C.** Find the volume of the cone.

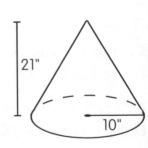

_____

**D.** Find the volume of the pyramid.

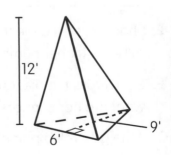

_____

Math • RB-904064

*Algebra*

Randy's older sister Ciara recently graduated from college. She applied for a job and was hired. Her new boss explained to her that the first decision she would need to make as a new employee would be how she wanted to receive her salary.

Her base starting salary will be $35,000.00. One option is to receive a pay raise of 3% after 1 year. She would get the same pay raise percentage after years 2 and 3. At the end of her fourth year, her percentage of pay increase will jump to 4%.

Her other option is to start at her base salary and receive $500.00 pay raises every 6 months. Ciara has asked Randy, "the family math whiz," to help her make a decision.

Weigh her options. Which is the better deal for Ciara? What advice would you give her. Explain your recommendation.

_____

_____

_____

_____

_____

_____

_____

Math • RB-904064

# LAZY EWE

Brad works at the Lazy Ewe Sheep Ranch. One of his jobs is to count the sheep in each flock. To count the sheep, Brad rents a helicopter once a year and takes photos of each flock. The camera then converts the photo into dots. Each dot represents one sheep. Brad then divides the pen into a grid that allows him to estimate the number of sheep in each section. His method is to choose a section that looks average for the entire field. He then counts the dots in that section and multiplies by the number of squares in the grid.

Look at the photo below of the dot pattern of sheep in one of the Lazy Ewe's pastures. Estimate the number of sheep in the flock by dividing the field into sections and then counting one section to make your estimate.

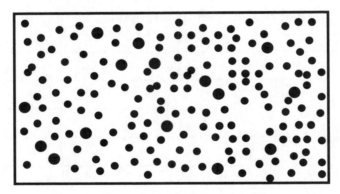

**A.** How many sheep do you estimate are in this pasture? _____

_____

**B.** How could you explain the area where there are no sheep at all?

_____

_____

**C.** Explain how you arrived at your answer. _____

_____

Math • RB-904064

*Number and Operations*

Since 2001, airport security all over the world has intensified. While the increased security is necessary to ensure safety in flying, it is not without its cost. Thousands of additional workers, sophisticated scanning machines, and other related costs have added billions of dollars to the cost of running an airport.

While governments and airlines have contributed much to the support of this added cost, passengers are now required to pay a security fee at each airport from which they initiate a flight. The add-on fee varies from one airport to another, but a typical fee is $10.00 to $15.00 per passenger per flight.

**A.** One airline advertises an Internet special for $92.09 one-way plus taxes and the security fee. The taxes are $16.21 and the security fee is $12.50. The return flight is the same cost for the ticket, but the taxes are $13.11 and the security fee is $11.00. What will be the total cost for this round-trip Internet special when all of the taxes and security fees are added onto the cost of the ticket?

---

**B.** What percent do the security fees account for in the round-trip cost of this trip? Round to the nearest whole percent.

---

**C.** At a major airport, the total traffic including arriving and departing passengers last year was 67,303,182. Of those, 33,836,077 were departing and 33,467,105 were arriving. If the passenger security fee at this airport for departing flights was $12.50 per passenger, how much revenue did this airport collect in security fees for the year?

---

Math • RB-904064

# USING A VENN DIAGRAM

Venn diagrams show similar characteristics and attributes among sets of objects.

**A.** A class of 22 students is polled about their pets at home. Nine students said that they have cats, and 13 students said that they have dogs. Four students have neither a cat nor a dog. How many students must have both cats and dogs?

_____

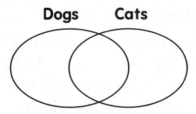

**Dogs     Cats**

**B.** Students in Mr. Robinson's science classes were asked whether they liked red sauce or white sauce on their pasta. The final results from the 126 students who responded to the poll are shown below. How many students must have said that they did not like either one?

_____

**White Sauce    Red Sauce**

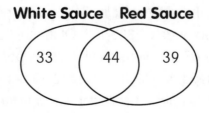

33    44    39

Math • RB-904064

*Geometry*

On the first day that Sammy went to survey school, he was taken to a plot of land with nine stakes arranged like the nine dots below. His first assignment was to mark off on the site as many triangles as he could find using colorful string.

At noon, Sammy showed his teacher the 31 triangles he had marked off. His teacher told him it was "a good first day in class." Can you find as many as Sammy? Perhaps you can find even more.

**Hint:** Draw several copies of the nine-dot pattern on another page or use colorful markers to show the different triangles.

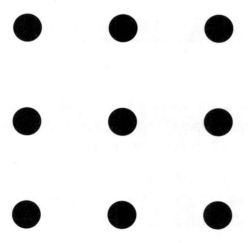

Count all of the triangles you found. Did you do as well as Sammy? Did you do even better? _____

_____

_____

_____

_____

© Rainbow Bridge Publishing

Math • RB-904064

The members of the Drama Club at Roosevelt Middle School decided to renovate the stage floor in the school auditorium. The semicircular section of the stage is centered on the rectangular section. Club members will first apply two coats of paint. Then, because there will be a lot of toe-tapping and stomping going on, they will give the floor a coat of clear sealer over the paint.

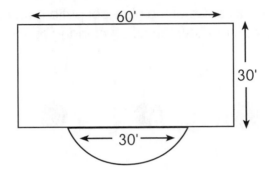

**A.** The clerk at the paint store said that 1 gallon of floor paint covers "roughly 90 square feet." How much paint does the Drama Club need to paint the floor of the stage twice? _____

**B.** The clear sealer they will apply over the paint requires a gallon of sealer per 75 square feet. How many gallons of sealer will they need to buy? _____

**C.** The salesman at Paint-to-Last told the treasurer of the Drama Club that the paint costs $14.00 per gallon, and the sealer is $24.00 per gallon. He also said that he would give them a 20% discount because the sale is to a school. There will not be any sales tax for the same reason. If they need $60.00 worth of brushes (also at a 20% discount), how much money will the Drama Club spend on renovating their stage floor?

_____

Math • RB-904064

# PAR FOR THE COURSE

## Number and Operations

In the game of golf, the object is to take as few strokes as possible to get the ball from the tee on each hole into the 4-inch cup hundreds of yards away. The golfer who takes the fewest strokes to complete all 18 holes in the round wins. Par is the standard used to determine the number of strokes a very skilled player should need on a particular hole. Totaling all of the pars for all 18 holes becomes the standard, or par, for the round.

The + signs and − signs on a golf scorecard are used to interpret each player's score relative to par. It is helpful to know some other golf terminology. An eagle is two strokes less than par. A birdie is one stroke less than par. A bogie on a hole is one stroke higher than par. Look at the scorecard below and answer the following questions.

| Hole | 1 | 2 | 3 | 4 | 5 | 6 | 7 | 8 | 9 | Total |
|------|---|---|---|---|---|---|---|---|---|-------|
| Par | 4 | 3 | 5 | 4 | 4 | 4 | 3 | 4 | 5 | 36 |
| Adams | E | E | −1 | −1 | E | E | E | E | −1 | |
| Hoch | E | E | E | E | E | −1 | E | E | E | |
| Pavin | +1 | E | E | +1 | +1 | +1 | +1 | +1 | +1 | |
| Hamilton | −1 | −1 | −2 | −2 | −1 | −1 | −1 | −2 | −3 | |

**A.** What score did Adams have on the 3rd hole?_____

**B.** What did Hoch have on the 1st hole? _____

**C.** Who had the best 9-hole score? _____

**D.** What score did Hamilton report for his 9-hole total? _____

**E.** Where did Adams get his birdies? _____

**F.** Who had the most pars in the round? _____

**G.** How many bogies did Pavin have during the round? _____

**H.** How many birdies did Hamilton have?_____

**I.** Which player had the highest score during the round?_____

**J.** How many strokes is Hamilton ahead of Hoch? _____

Math • RB-904064

# BURNING CALORIES

Exercise contributes to good health and physical fitness. Different levels of exercise burn different numbers of calories. The time spent and the body weight of the person exercising are also factored into the number of calories burned.

Use the equations below to find answers. In each equation, C equals the number of calories burned. W is the number of pounds greater than 100 of the person exercising. Since 30 minutes is a common time length for exercise, that number does not need to be included in the equations.

Jogging: $C = 1.6(W) + 158$
Jumping Rope: $C = 2.1(W) + 220$
Hiking: $C = 1.4(W) + 136$
Low-Impact Aerobics: $C = 1.1(W) + 114$
Swimming: $C = 1.8(W) + 182$
Walking Briskly: $C = 0.8(W) + 180$

**A.** Chris weighs 118 pounds. How many calories did he burn in a 30-minute jog? _____

**B.** If Gretchen weighs 102 pounds and swims for 30 minutes, how many calories will she burn?_____

**C.** Evie's dad weighs 220 pounds. He went for a brisk 30-minute walk. How many calories did he burn? _____

**D.** Andy's older brother Homer weighs 160 pounds. How many calories will Homer burn by jumping rope for 30 minutes? _____

 Math • RB-904064

*Algebra*

A local health club called Fitness Plus offers a plan for students under 18 in which they pay a monthly fee of $10.00 plus $3.00 each time they use the facility. Make a list to show what it will cost to use the facilities at Fitness Plus for up to 8 times a month.

| Times Used | Computation | Total Cost |
|:----------:|:-----------:|:----------:|
| 0 | $10 + 3(0) = 10$ | $10.00 |
| 1 | | |
| 2 | | |
| 3 | | |
| 4 | | |
| 5 | | |
| 6 | | |
| 7 | | |
| 8 | | |

Use this information to write an expression that could be used to find the cost in each case without constructing the list.

_____

Health World, a similar health club a few blocks away, also offers a "Youth Plan." There is no monthly fee, but the club charges $5.00 each time the facility is used. Fill in the chart below to compare the fees and number of times used. On the line below, write a statement that tells when it would be better to be a member of Fitness Plus and when it would be better to work out at Health World.

| Times Used | 0 | 1 | 2 | 3 | 4 | 5 | 6 | 7 | 8 |
|:----------:|:-:|:-:|:-:|:-:|:-:|:-:|:-:|:-:|:-:|
| Fitness Plus | 10 | 13 | | | | | | | |
| Health World | 0 | 5 | | | | | | | |

_____

© Rainbow Bridge Publishing     Math • RB-904064

Complete the diagrams.

**A.** Using this pool of numbers, decide where to place them in the Venn diagram below. First, label each circle. Then, position each number inside the Venn diagram so that it satisfies the label for that circle.

1, 2, 3, 4, 5, 6, 7, 8, 9, 10, 11, 12, 13, 14, 15, 16

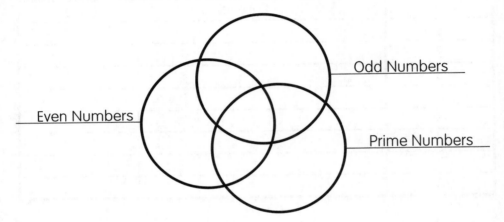

Odd Numbers

Even Numbers

Prime Numbers

**B.** Use the same strategy for this group of numbers.

2, 6, 12, 15, 18, 20, 21, 24, 27, 28, 30, 32, 33, 36, 39

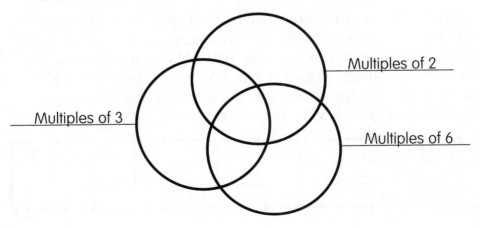

Multiples of 2

Multiples of 3

Multiples of 6

Math • RB-904064

*Measurement, Number and Operations*

Joni's parents are allowing her to redecorate her bedroom. Her room measures 12' x 14'. The ceiling in her room is 8' high.

**A.** Since she is starting from the top and working her way down, she will first paint the ceiling. She only needs to paint the ceiling one time. If a quart of paint covers 100 square feet, how much paint should she buy to cover the ceiling?

_____

**B.** Joni plans to give the walls two coats of paint. She will be using a different color paint than she used on the ceiling. Below, explain how you would determine the amount of paint Joni should buy to paint the walls in her room.

_____

_____

_____

**C.** Joni wants a decorative border around the top of the room. The border she wants is sold only by the yard. How many yards will she need for her room?

_____

**D.** Finally, it's time for the carpet. The carpet that Joni chooses costs $32.00 per square yard and includes the carpet pad and the installation. How much will it cost to carpet Joni's room? Round to the nearest whole dollar.

_____

Math • RB-904064

*Measurement, Geometry*

Answer the questions.

**A.** A tree that is 10' tall casts a shadow of 7'. A nearby building casts a shadow of 28'. How tall is the building in feet? _____

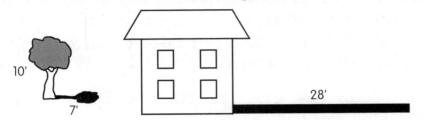

**B.** Look at the parallelogram below. What is the measure of the angle ∠CDE? _____

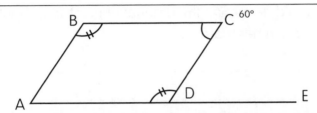

**C.** Melanie can run the 100-yard dash in 12.0 seconds. What is her speed in feet per minute? Round her speed to the nearest 100 feet per minute. _____

**D.** A small model of the Statue of Liberty measures 10". If 1" = 30', what is the height of the statue? _____

**E.** Each shape below has a volume of 48 cubic inches. Which of the shapes has the greatest surface area? Circle the letter of your choice.

**a.**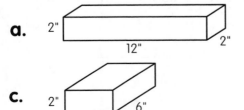

**b.**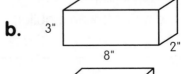

**c.** 

**d.**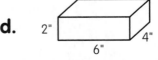

# MAKING GUESSTIMATES

*Measurement*

A *guesstimate* is an estimate that is made using common sense and logic. Make guesstimates for each of the questions below. Record your guesstimates. Then, check them to see how close you were.

**A.** How many blades of grass are in a square inch of lawn?

My guesstimate:_____    The actual answer: _____

**B.** How many swallows of a soft drink are in a 12-ounce can?

My guesstimate:_____    The actual answer: _____

**C.** How many kernels of popcorn are in a cup?

My guesstimate:_____    The actual answer: _____

**D.** In a half-hour television program, how many minutes are devoted to the actual show?

My guesstimate:_____    The actual answer: _____

**E.** How many of your steps does it take to walk the length of a football field?

My guesstimate:_____    The actual answer: _____

**F.** How many minutes of class time are left in this school year?

My guesstimate:_____    The actual answer: _____

Which of your guesstimates came closest to being accurate? _____

Which of your guesstimates missed the mark by the greatest margin?

_____

© Rainbow Bridge Publishing                      Math • RB-904064

*Data Analysis*

Mr. Green's home had the most beautiful lawn on the block, without a weed or dandelion. His neighbors marveled at his lawn and asked him for advice on making their own lawns better. In the past, he fertilized his lawn four times each year and aerated it every fall and every spring.

Mr. Green's property measures 215' x 180'. His house occupies 2,400 square feet, his garage another 900 square feet, and his driveway 1,080 square feet. A small storage shed in the corner of the backyard measures 12' x 10'.

In the fall, he used a longer-lasting fertilizer. He bought a bag of fertilizer that covers 20,000 square feet for $32.00, another that covers 10,000 square feet for $18.00, and a bag that covers 5,000 square feet for $12.00.

For each of his other three fertilizer applications, he bought a bag that covers 20,000 square feet for $28.00, a bag that covers 10,000 square feet for $15.00, and a bag that covers 5,000 square feet for $10.00. He also rented an aerator for $50.00 per day twice a year. Mr. Green plans to eliminate his spring aeration and cut out the mid-summer application of fertilizer.

**A.** How much money did Mr. Green spend on his lawn-beautification program per year in the past?

_____

**B.** How much does he plan to spend this year?_____

**C.** What percent will Mr. Green save this year over his expenses in the past? Round to the nearest whole percent. _____

Math • RB-904064

*Data Analysis*

Rather than interpreting data, create data to fit the conditions described in each situation. Show your work to prove that you have chosen valid data.

**A.** Create a set of data that contains 11 test scores that satisfies each condition below:

Mean: 83 _____

Median: 81 _____

Mode: 80 _____

Range: 26 _____

**B.** Create a set of data showing temperature highs for 10 days that satisfies each condition below:

Mean: 72° _____

Median: 74° _____

Mode: 68° _____

Range: 21° _____

**C.** Create a list of batting averages that satisfies the nine-member baseball team's data below:

Mean: 0.237 _____

Median: 0.231 _____

Mode: 0.237 _____

Range: 0.126 _____

Math • RB-904064

As in all sports, numbers play a key role in the game of basketball. The most important numbers are, of course, the points at the end of the game. However, many other numbers are important to basketball and help define the game.

Each piece of basketball information below is represented by a letter. Substitute the **boldfaced** values for the letters to solve the equations. Then, circle true or false.

A = During a basketball game, **10** players can be on the court.

B = The rim is **10'** above the court.

C = The length of halftime in both college and professional games is **15** minutes.

D = **Five** fouls will disqualify a player from further play in a college game.

E = **Ninety-four** feet is the length of a basketball court.

F = A bonus is awarded after the **7**th foul in each half of a college game.

G = Double **0** is the lowest number that can appear on a player's jersey.

H = There are **24** seconds on the shot clock in professional basketball.

I = **Fifty** feet is the width of a basketball court.

J = A game ball's maximum weight is **650** grams.

**A.** $(C - D) - A = G$
　　True　　False

**B.** $(E - H) \div B = F$
　　True　　False

**C.** $(H - F) + D = H$
　　True　　False

**D.** $A \times (I + B) + I = J$
　　True　　False

**E.** $C \div (A \div B) - F = D$
　　True　　False

**F.** $F + (J \div I) + D = H$
　　True　　False

　　　Math • RB-904064

*Measurement*

**A.** Randy is mailing a birthday gift to his sister Raylene. The present he bought does not come close to fitting into the 10 cm x 12 cm x 6 cm box he has. In fact, his mother told him that he needs a box twice the size. Explain the various sizes of boxes he might use to measure up to his mother's words.

_____

_____

_____

_____

What factors will determine which of the choices he actually uses?

_____

_____

_____

**B.** Cheryl went to the closest We Mail Anywhere store to buy a box. The standard size box for mailing measures 9" x 12" x 6" and holds 648 cubic inches. The clerk said that he had boxes that measured twice the size of each of the dimensions for the standard box. He asked Cheryl if she wanted one dimension doubled, two dimensions doubled, or did she need a box that had all three dimensions doubled?

Calculate and explain her choices. Then, decide which box you would suggest that she buy.

_____

_____

_____

_____

Math • RB-904064

It is sometimes useful to create a rough diagram to help solve math problems. Solving problems like these becomes much simpler if you use a diagram.

**A.** French doors that lead to a patio behind a house are both made of glass panes. Each door has 3 vertical columns of panes with 6 rows in each column. Each pane measures 6" horizontally x 10" vertically. Each row and column has $1\frac{1}{2}$" wooden dividers between the panes of glass. There is a wooden frame surrounding the glass that measures $5\frac{1}{2}$" per side. What are the outside measurements of the French doors that lead to the patio?

**B.** Draw two straight lines to divide the numbers on the face of a clock into 3 sections so that the numbers in each section add up to the same sum.

*Probability*

The odds of winning an event can be calculated by comparing the ratio of the favorable outcomes to the total number of possible outcomes. Use this information to answer the questions.

**A.** What are the odds of drawing a vowel from a bag containing two sets of tiles with letters of the alphabet? (Consider the letter *y* as a consonant.) _____

**B.** What are the odds of drawing one of the letters in the word *winner* from a bag containing one tile with each letter of the alphabet on it?

_____

**C.** What are the odds of drawing one of the letters in your last name from the same bag that contains one tile for each letter of the alphabet? _____

**D.** Using a standard deck of 52 playing cards, what are your odds of drawing a 2? _____

**E.** Using a standard deck of playing cards, what are your odds of drawing a face card?_____

**F.** Using a standard deck of playing cards, what are the odds of drawing an ace of spades if your playing partner just drew an ace of diamonds and he is still holding his card?_____

**G.** If you draw a 4 of hearts from a standard deck of playing cards and then draw a 6 of hearts from the same deck on your next draw, what are the odds that you will draw yet another heart on your third draw? (You do not replace the two cards already drawn.)

_____

Math • RB-904064

Answer the questions. Circle the number of each true statement.

**A.** A daily lottery game advertises "1 winner for every 4 players." If this statement is true, which of the following statements are also true?

  **1.** Twenty-five of every 100 players will be winners.
  **2.** For every 3 winners, there is 1 loser.
  **3.** Someone standing behind three people who all buy losing lottery tickets will be a winner.
  **4.** If 40 people buy lottery tickets, 10 of them can be expected to be winners.

**B.** Drawing from a standard deck of 52 cards leads to the following probabilities:

  **1.** The probability of drawing a red card is 1 in 2.
  **2.** The probability of drawing an ace is 1 in 13.
  **3.** The probability of drawing a 3 of clubs is 1 in 26.
  **4.** The probability of drawing a face card is 1 in 10.

**C.** A bag contains the following marbles: 5 yellow, 10 blue, 6 red, 8 clear, and 7 green. Which of the following statements are true?

  **1.** The probability of drawing a blue marble from the bag is greater than drawing a yellow, red, clear, or green marble from the bag.
  **2.** The probability of drawing a red or blue marble is better than 1 in 2.
  **3.** The probability of drawing either a green or clear marble is 5 in 12.
  **4.** The probability of drawing a yellow, blue, or green marble is better than 2 in 3.

*Data Analysis*

Data is used on a daily basis to make important decisions. Learning to analyze data and drawing logical conclusions from the presentation of data is one of the goals of math education.

Look at the scatter plot diagram below. Without any other details available, study what you see and jot down four statements you can make about the data presented.

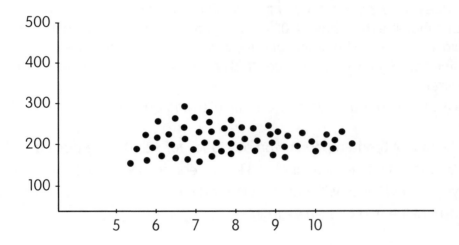

1. _____

2. _____

3. _____

4. _____

Where do you think this data might have been gathered?

_____

_____

_____

 Math • RB-904064

Investors and economists constantly watch the rate of inflation. In fact, the rate of inflation is so important to some people that they base most of their financial decisions on the state of the economy. If the rate of inflation goes up, then today's dollar will not buy as much as it would have bought yesterday. For example, if the inflation rate is 3%, then a loaf of bread that cost $2.00 last year now costs 103% of $2.00, or $2.06.

That may not sound like much. However, if everything a person buys and does costs 3% more today than it did last year at this time, that means that she must have $103.00 for every $100.00 she had last year just to stay even. If she does not have that extra $3.00, then she cannot buy the same goods and services that she was able to buy last year at this time.

Use this information to answer the following questions.

**A.** If a loaf of bread a person can buy today for $2.00 undergoes a "rate-of-inflation-price-hike" of 3% per year each year for the next 10 years, how much will that loaf of bread cost? Round to the nearest cent at the end of each year. _____

**B.** If the current rate of inflation remains at 2.5% for five years in succession, what will a new car that currently costs $20,000.00 cost in five years? Round to the nearest whole dollar at the end of each year.

**C.** If an employee who begins working at a salary of $35,000.00 per year has a clause in his contract that "guarantees 4% raises per year for each of his first 5 years," how much will his salary be to start his 6th year? Round to the nearest whole dollar at the end of each year. _____

Math • RB-904064

*Data Analysis*

One way to express a changed amount is by stating the change as a percentage increase or decrease. For example, if you see a shirt that was originally priced at $20.00 now being offered for sale at $14.00, you would save $6.00. Another way to express your savings would be to divide the savings ($6.00) by the original price ($20.00). The shirt is being sold at a 30% discount off the original price.

For each of the following questions, indicate both the amount of change and the percentage change of the increase or decrease.

**A.** The price of gasoline dropped from $1.70 per gallon to $1.53 in less than a month.

Amount:_____          Percentage:_____

**B.** Anna's father received a salary increase from $39,000.00 to $40,560.00.

Amount:_____          Percentage:_____

**C.** The size of the glass needed to cover a picture increased significantly when the original 8" x 10" photo was enlarged to an 11" x 14" photo.

Amount:_____          Percentage:_____

**D.** The city council reduced the annual budget from $24.5 million to $22 million in a single year.

Amount:_____          Percentage:_____

**E.** The Internet provider lost 2 million subscribers in a single year and now has only 24.7 million left.

Amount:_____          Percentage:_____

Math • RB-904064

The Pythagorean theorem states that the square of the hypotenuse of a right triangle is equal to the sum of the squares of the other two sides of the triangle.

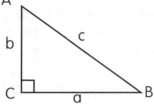

Study the chart showing some combinations that make the formula for the Pythagorean Theorem true: $a^2 + b^2 = c^2$. Fill in the missing numbers on the chart.

| a | b | c |
|---|---|---|
| 3 | 4 | 5 |
| 5 |   | 13 |
| 7 | 24 |   |
|   | 15 | 17 |
| 9 |   | 41 |

Describe the patterns you see in the relationship of the combinations of numbers to each other.

_____

_____

_____

How could this information be helpful to you in the future with problems you face concerning the Pythagorean theorem?

_____

_____

_____

Math • RB-904064

# DISCOUNT CARPET WORLD

*Measurement*

Andy Anderson and his parents are excited about their new home. Before they move in, the Andersons plan to replace some of the carpeting. Andy and his dad measured the rooms they want to recarpet, and they all headed to Carl's Carpet World. They agreed on carpeting that cost $34.00 per square yard. The price included the carpet pad and the installation.

Using the dimensions for each area, determine the number of square feet of carpeting needed. Convert that number to square yards and determine the cost for each area. Can the Andersons carpet the areas that need new carpeting for under $3,000.00?

### Living Room

13.5' x 18.5'

Square feet: _____

Square yards: _____

Cost: _____

### Master Bedroom

16' x 15'

Square feet: _____

Square yards: _____

Cost: _____

### Andy's Bedroom

11.5' x 13.5'

Square feet: _____

Square yards: _____

Cost: _____

### Main Hallway

6.5' x 3.5'

Square feet: _____

Square yards: _____

Cost: _____

### Hallway to Andy's Room

6.5' x 3.5'

Square feet: _____

Square yards: _____

Cost: _____

### Closets (3)

All closets measure 6.5' x 5'

Square feet: _____

Square yards: _____

Cost: _____

**Total Cost:** _____

© Rainbow Bridge Publishing

Math • RB-904064

# TACO STIX

Marketing research firms often gather data on consumer preferences to help predict how well new products will sell. Manufacturers are willing to pay for this research because it costs a lot of money to produce, advertise, and sell a product on a national basis. If the data is collected carefully and the research is valid, the opinions of the people polled will give the manufacturer a fairly good idea of how well the product will sell.

Due to the popularity of low-carbohydrate diets, a company developed a taco-flavored stick that is carbohydrate-free. The company hired a research consultant to find out if the public would like Taco Stix, the name they plan to use. Look at the data collected from a consumer preference survey conducted in five western regions.
Use the data to answer the questions.

| Age | Liked Taco Stix | Disliked Taco Stix |
|---|---|---|
| 8–15 | 124 | 76 |
| 16–26 | 163 | 37 |
| 27–36 | 113 | 87 |
| 36–47 | 127 | 73 |
| 48–60 | 119 | 81 |

**A.** How many people were included in this survey?_____

**B.** Which age group liked Taco Stix best? _____

**C.** Did any age group not like Taco Stix? _____

**D.** What percentage of the sample surveyed liked Taco Stix? Round to the nearest tenth of a percent. _____

**E.** Using the statistics collected from this survey, how many people would you expect to like Taco Stix from a group of 10,000 people who range in age from 16 to 26 years? _____

**F.** Based on this survey, do you think it would be a wise decision by the executives of the company to launch Taco Stix nationwide? Why or why not?

_____

Math • RB-904064

*Probability*

Answer the questions.

**A.** A bag containing colorful tiles includes the following: 14 blue, 12 red, 18 yellow, 6 green. Which of the following statements is true? Circle the number of the true statement.

    **I.** There is a better chance of drawing a yellow or green tile than drawing a blue or red tile.

    **2.** The chance of drawing a yellow tile is 36%.

    **3.** The chance of drawing a yellow tile is twice as great as the chance of drawing a green one.

    **4.** The chance of drawing a green tile is less than 1 in 10.

**B.** Using the same bag of colorful tiles, what is the probability that the first tile drawn will NOT be blue?

_____

**C.** What is the probability that you could roll a 1 on a die and draw an ace from a standard deck of 52 playing cards? Show all of your calculations in arriving at your answer.

_____

**D.** If you roll a pair of dice, what is the probability that the total would be greater than 5? Show all of your calculations in arriving at your answer.

_____

Math • RB-904064

# ANSWER KEY

## P. 4-6 — ASSESSMENT TEST
A. 3.  B. 3.  C. 3.  D. 4.
E. 2.  F. 1.  G. 3.  H. 2.
I. 4.  J. 3.  K. 3.

## P. 8 — PRIME TIME
The 25 prime numbers less than 100 are:
2, 3, 5, 7, 11, 13, 17, 19, 23, 29, 31, 37, 41, 43,
47, 53, 59, 61, 67, 71, 73, 79, 83, 89, 97. There
are 25 prime numbers less than 100.

## P. 9 — TILE TURNOVERS
A. toothbrush  B. strawberry  C. scoreboard
D. recreation  E. laboratory  F. delightful
Patterns include the first two letters of each
word being on a tile that is upside down, and
the words are presented in reverse order of
being alphabetized.

## P. 10 — PICTURE THIS!
A. 9 in.$^2$   B. 7 in.$^2$   C. 9.8 in.$^2$
D. The area is the sum of the two widths.
E. 12 in.$^2$   F. 15 in.$^2$   G. 19 in.$^2$
H. Answers will vary.

## P. 11 — ODDS ARE
A. 4:11; 8:11   B. 3:6
C. 7:9   D. 2:13

## P. 12 — BEAR CANYON
A. 20 miles   B. 1,375 yd.
C. 1,250 yd.   D. 3,000 yd.

## P. 13 — SOLID VIEWS
A. 1   B. 2
C.
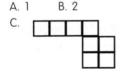

## P. 14 — ORDER OF OPERATIONS
Order of operations: parenthesis; exponents;
multiplication/division (from left to right);
addition/subtraction (from left to right)
A. 14  B. 30  C. 33  D. -1  E. 11
F. 3  G. 324  H. 188  I. 18  J. -3
K. 6  L. 24  M. 5  N. 50  O. 8.8
P. -.4  Q. 6  R. 3

## P. 15 — NUMBER SLEUTH
A. 5, 5  B. 1, 5  C. -2, -3  D. 18, 3
E. -8, 24  F. -4, 1  G. 6, -6  H. 3, 9

## P. 16 — WHAT IS THAT NUMBER?
A. 107  B. 27  C. 83  D. 84
E. 26  F. 88  G. 43  H. 36
I. 121  J. 139

## P. 17 — WHAT'S MISSING?

## P. 18 — TEETER-TOTTER
A. 60 in.  B. 42 in.  C. 130 lb.  D. 42 in.

## P. 19 — KEYPAD COMMUNICATIONS
A. Iceland  B. Germany
C. England  D. Jamaica
E. 1-800-GOGLASS  F. 1-800-TAXHELP

## P. 20 — RATIO RUNDOWN
A. 17:12  B. 12:29  C. 17:29
D. 1:2  E. 1:2  F. all three choices

## P. 21 — GRETCHEN'S GARDEN
A. 360 seeds
B. Plot sizes may vary, but should contain
108 ft.$^2$ to accommodate 20 plants that
are 36 in. from each other. A 9' x 12'
arrangement is one possibility.
C. Plot sizes may vary, but should contain
18 ft.$^2$ to accommodate 15 plants that
are 18 in. from each other. A 3' x 6'
arrangement is one possibility.

## P. 22 — ANNIE'S NEW PHONE
Spider Cellular: 0 minutes = $29.95,
100 minutes = $29.95, 200 minutes = $29.95,
300  minutes = $49.95
Stay-In-Touch: 0 minutes = $0.00
100 minutes = $15.00, 200 minutes = $30.00,
300 minutes = $45.00
Cristini Wireless: 0 minutes = $19.95,
100 minutes = $19.95, 200 minutes = $39.95,
300 minutes = 59.95
Annie's best plan for 300 minutes per month
is with the Stay-in-Touch plan in which she
pays $0.15 per minute.

## P. 23 — SUPPLIER OF THE MULTIPLIER
Horizontal row blanks:  first row - $\frac{1}{2}$, $\frac{2}{3}$
third row - $\frac{2}{3}$, $\frac{1}{2}$  fifth row - $\frac{1}{12}$, 18

76

## P. 24 — SCHOOL SHOPPING
A. $89.00    B. $178.00    C. $667.50
D. $237.00 (including lunch, tip, and CD)

## P. 25 — SHADY ESTIMATES
A. 25%    B. 40%    C. 40%
Answers will vary for D, E, and F but should be shaded per instructions.

## P. 26 — UNEQUAL PORTIONS
1. A. 20%   B. 30%   C. 45%   D. 5%
2. A. 10%   B. 20%   C. 20%   D. 30%
   E. 20%
3. A. 25%   B. 40%   C. 25%   D. 10%
4. A. 17%   B. 32%   C. 17%   D. 17%
   E. 17%
5. A. 50%   B. 25%   C. 12.5%  D. 12.5%
6. A. 50%   B. 30%   C. 15%   D. 5%

## P. 27 — WHAT'S IN THE MIDDLE?
A. 5 - Subtract the top two numbers. Subtract the bottom two numbers. Then, subtract the difference.
B. 6 - Divide the top two numbers. Divide the bottom two numbers. Multiply the two quotients.
C. 12 - Multiply the top two numbers. Add the bottom two numbers. Subtract the bottom sum from the top product.

## P. 28 — I'M THINKING OF NUMBERS
A. 3, 9    B. 6, 12    C. 4, 3    D. 12, 18
E. 12, -2    F. -8, -16    G. -4, -2    H. 15, 8

## P. 29 — EQUATION BUILDING
A. $6x + 5 = 3x + 14$    B. $3x - 8 = 7$
C. $x \div 3 + 4 = 9$

## P. 30 — CAMP SAUKENAUK

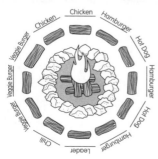

## P. 31 — THE BEST GRAPH
A. bar graph    B. circle graph
C. line graph    D. line graph    E. bar graph

## P. 32 — ANNUAL SALES MEETING
A. 35              B. 6 cars

## P. 33 — CONOVER CANS
A. $V = 63$ in.$^3$
B. $V = 157$ in.$^3$
C. The container would need to be approx. 12.5 inches high.
D. Answers will vary. The container would need to be slightly larger than 48 inches high, 5 inches wide, and 5 inches long.

## P. 34 — COMPARING SURFACE AREAS
A. 1,507.2 cm$^2$        B. 45        C. 13

## P. 35 — BIG CITY LIVING
A. Phoenix  B. Detroit
1. +1.0%    2. +2.8%    3. -0.3%    4. +2.9%
5. -1.7%    6. +3.8%    7. +3.0%    8. +1.9%
9. +3.7%   10. -2.8%

## P. 36 — ESTIMATION STATION
Answers will vary.

## P. 37 — HANNA'S HORSE ARENA
A. The rope needs to be approximately 50' long.
B. $2,669.00
C. She can accommodate 10 horses.

## P. 38 — THE PYTHAGOREAN TRIPLE
A. 13"        B. 24"        C. 25"
D. 12"        E. 4"         F. 6"

## P. 39 — SQUARE DEAL
A. The counting by 5s begins in lower left corner and proceeds counterclockwise around the square and continues to work toward the center.
B. Counting in horizontal rows is by 10s. All vertical rows involve counting by 2. Horizontal rows involve counting by 10.

Math • RB-904064

# ANSWER KEY

## P. 40 — MEETING LINES
A. parallel          B. perpendicular
C. acute   D. right   E. obtuse   F. F
G. F       H. F       I. T         J. F

## P. 41 — COULD IT BE?
A. F       B. F       C. F
D. F       E. Possibly true        F. F
G. F       H. T       I. F         J. T

## P. 42 — FASTEST-GROWING CITIES
Chula Vista          rank 7    11.7% increase
Chandler             rank 4    14.4% increase
North Las Vegas      rank 2    17.7% increase
Joliet               rank 9    11.4% increase
Gilbert              rank 1    22.8% increase
Fontana              rank 9    11.4% increase
Henderson            rank 3    17.2% increase
Peoria               rank 5    13.4% increase
Rancho Cucamonga     rank 7    11.7% increase
Irvine               rank 6    13.3% increase

Conclusions include that fastest growing cities are in the West. Arizona, California, and Nevada account for 9 of the 10 fastest growing cities.

## P. 43 — COORDINATE LANGUAGE
A. x-axis   B. y-axis   C. origin   D. 4, 4
E. 3 units   F. right triangle
G. scalene triangle

## P. 44 — STAIRWAY TO THE STARS
A. $5,940 \text{ in.}^2$   B. $41.25 \text{ ft.}^2$   C. $525.94
D. $144.38   E. $670.32

## P. 45 — MATTERS OF PROPORTION
A. $0.40     B. $3.00     C. $12.50
D. $12.00    E. 81

## P. 46 — MAKING SENSE
A. yes     B. yes     C. no      D. no
E. yes     F. no      G. yes     H. yes
I. yes     J. yes     K. yes     L. yes

## P. 47 — CHANCES ARE
A. 1 in 9    B. 4 in 9    C. 5 in 9 over 4 in 9
D. 5 in 6    E. 1 in 2    F. 1 in 6    G. 1 in 36

## P. 48 — VOLUMES AND VOLUMES
A. $66 \text{ in.}^3$     B. $384 \text{ ft.}^3$
C. $2,200 \text{ in.}^3$  D. $108 \text{ ft.}^3$

## P. 49 — CIARA'S SALARY
The second option is only a few dollars better for Ciara as she would make $187,500.00 in salary during the first five years. The first option would give her total earnings of $186,202.22 for the first five years. She needs to ask if the percentage offered will continue to grow as she continues to work for the company before making her decision.

## P. 50 — LAZY EWE
Answers will vary. Explanation could be standing water in the area or steep terrain.

## P. 51 — HIGH COST OF SAFETY
A. $237.00 B. 10%     C. $422,950,962.50

## P. 52 — USING A VENN DIAGRAM
A. Four students have both a cat and a dog.
B. Ten students said they didn't like either red sauce or white sauce.

## P. 53 — SURVEY SCHOOL
There are at least 31 triangles that can be constructed from the 9 stakes.

## P. 54 — PAINT-TO-LAST
A. 48 gallons   B. 29 gallons   C. $1,142.40

## P. 55 — PAR FOR THE COURSE
A. 4       B.  4      C. Hamilton   D. 22
E. #3, #4, and #9      F.  Hoch       G. 7
H. 5       I.  Pavin   J.  13

## P. 56 — BURNING CALORIES
A. 186.8 calories       B. 185.6 calories
C. 276 calories         D. 346 calories

Math • RB-904064

# ANSWER KEY

## p. 57 – FITNESS PLUS

Total cost = 10 + 3n. Anyone using the facilities fewer than 5 times per month should go to Health World. Five visits results in the same price at both places. Any number of visits over 5 would make Fitness Plus a better deal.
Computations and costs are as follows:

0 visits: 10 + 3(0) = $13.00
1 visit: 10 + 3(1) = $16.00
2 visits: 10 + 3(2) = $16.00
3 visits: 10 + 3(3) = $19.00
4 visits: 10 + 3(4) = $22.00
5 visits: 10 + 3(5) = $25.00
6 visits: 10 + 3(6) = $28.00
7 visits: 10 + 3(7) = $31.00
8 visits: 10 + 3(8) = $34.00

Costs per visit at Health Word are as follows:
0 visits = $0.00, 1 visit = $5.00, 2 visits = $10.00,
3 visits = $15.00, 4 visits = $20.00,
5 visits = $25.00, 6 visits = $30.00,
7 visits = $35.00, 8 visits = $40.00

## p. 58 – CLASSIFYING NUMBERS

A. Odd numbers are 1, 9, 15; even numbers are 4, 6, 8, 10, 12, 14, 16; the number 2 should be displayed in both the prime and even number parts of the diagram; the numbers 3, 5, 7, 11, and 13 should be displayed in both the odd and prime number parts of the diagram.
B. Multiples of 2 only include 2, 20, 28, and 32; Multiples of 3 only include 15, 21, 27, 33, and 39; the numbers 6, 12, 18, 24, 30, and 36 should be in the portions of the diagram that shows their being multiples of 2, 3, and 6.
Students may classify numbers in various ways. Accept any reasonable answers.

## p. 59 – JONI'S ROOM

A. 2 quarts
B. She should buy 2 gallons of paint and 1 quart of paint if it is sold by the quart.
C. She will need to buy 18 yards of border.
D. $597

## p. 60 – MEASUREMENT MATTERS

A. 40'    B. 60°    C. 1,500' per minute
D. 300'    E. a.

## p. 61 – MAKING GUESSTIMATES

Answers will vary.

## p. 62 – BEST ON THE BLOCK

A. $321.00    B. $218.00    C. 32%

## p. 63 – CREATING DATA

Answers will vary.

## p. 64 – A GAME OF NUMBERS

A. True   B. True   C. False
D. True   E. False   F. False

## p. 65 – TWICE THE SIZE

A. 20 x 12 x 6 cm; 10 x 24 x 6 cm; 10 x 12 x 12 cm are all dimensions that will work. The size and shape of the gift he wants to mail and the size of the available boxes that will accommodate the package are all factors he should consider.
B. She could buy either the 9" x 24" x 6" box or the 18" x 12" x 12" box. Her preference should depend on the shape of the gift she is sending.

## p. 66 – DRAW YOUR OWN DIAGRAM

A. Outside measurements of the doors are 64" wide x 78.5" high.
B. One line should be drawn to include the numbers 11, 12, 1, and 2. Another should include the numbers 9, 10, 3, and 4. That will leave the final portion of the clock to include the numbers 5, 6, 7, and 8. All portions have numbers that add up to 26.

## p. 67 – ODDS OF WINNING

A. 5:21    B. 5:21
C. Answers will vary.  D. 4:52 or 1:13
E. 12:52 or 3:13    F. 1:51
G. 11:50

## p. 68 – PROBABLE CAUSE

A. 1, 4    B. 1, 2    C. 1, 3

© Rainbow Bridge Publishing    Math • RB-904064

## p. 69 — Decisions from Data

Answers will vary, but four statements that can be made include:

1. The data began after 5.
2. No data was collected after 9.
3. The heaviest concentration of data was between 5 and 7.
4. The vertical concentration of data extended between 100 and 300.

## p. 70 — Inflation Station

A.  now - $2.00          year 2 - $2.06
    year 3 - $2.12        year 4 - $2.18
    year 5 - $2.25        year 6 - $2.32
    year 7 - $2.39        year 8 - $2.46
    year 9 - $2.53        year 10 - $2.61

B.  now - $20,000.00      year 2 - $20,500.00
    year 3 - $21,013.00   year 4 - $21,538.00
    year 5 - $22,076.00

C.  now - $35,000.00      year 2 - $36,400.00
    year 3 - $37,856.00   year 4 - $39,370.00
    year 5 - $40,945.00

## p. 71 — Percentage Change

A. Decrease is $0.17, a 10% drop.
B. Increase is $1,560.00, a 4% increase in pay.
C. Increased area of glass is 74 in.$^2$, a 92.5% increase.
D. Budget is reduced by $2.5 million, a 10.2% reduction in the budget.
E. The Internet provider lost 2 million subscribers, a decrease of 7.5% in subscribers.

## p. 72 — Pythagorean Patterns

| a | b | c |
|---|---|---|
| 3 | 4 | 5 |
| 5 | 12 | 13 |
| 7 | 24 | 25 |
| 8 | 15 | 17 |
| 9 | 40 | 41 |

Patterns include the following:
If a is odd, then b + 1 = c. If a is even, then b + 2 = c.
This information could serve as a useful check on the accuracy of the work. It could also save time in figuring square roots if two sides of the right triangle are known.

## p. 73 — Discount Carpet World

Living room - $943.50
Master bedroom - $906.67
Andy's bedroom - $586.50
Main hallway - $86.02
Hallway to Andy's room - $86.02
Closets - $368.22
Total cost: $2,976.93

## p. 74 — Taco Stix

A. 1,000     B. 16–26     C. no     D. 64.6%
E. 8,150 people          F. Answers will vary.

## p. 75 — Probability Prospects

A. 2     B. $\frac{18}{25}$     C. $\frac{1}{78}$     D. $\frac{13}{18}$

Math • RB-904064